Ohio's Covered Bridges

ISLAND RUN (HELMICK MILL) COVERED BRIDGE IN MORGAN COUNTY. The author, Elma Lee Moore, is pictured here at the Island Run Covered Bridge in October 2009.

ON THE FRONT COVER: This winter scene is beautifully reflected in the waters of Mill Creek. Eagleville or Foreman Road Covered Bridge (35-04-17) was built in Ashtabula County in 1862. Its fate was different than most. In 1972, it was dismantled and the timbers incorporated into a pizza parlor.

ON THE BACK COVER: The Duncan Falls Covered Bridge (35-60-47) in Muskingum County was built in 1864. A lock and canal can be seen in the foreground. The iron bridge pivoted to allow canal boats to travel through the lock. The center of the postcard shows the dam on the river. Remnants of locks and sections of the canal can still be seen along the river. The covered bridge was washed away in the great flood of 1913.

POSTCARD HISTORY SERIES

Ohio's Covered Bridges

Elma Lee Moore

ARCADIA
PUBLISHING

Published by Arcadia Publishing
Charleston, South Carolina

Printed in the United States of America

Library of Congress Control Number: 2009942519

For all general information contact Arcadia Publishing at:
Telephone 843-853-2070
Fax 843-853-0044
E-mail sales@arcadiapublishing.com
For customer service and orders:
Toll-Free 1-888-313-2665

Visit us on the Internet at www.arcadiapublishing.com

In memory of my mother, Daisy Hally Morris Patterson Schmidt, who grew up by Island Run Covered Bridge and inspired this book.

CONTENTS

ACKNOWLEDGMENTS

I am appreciative of my loving family, friends, and coworkers who gave me the support and confidence to write this book. I am grateful for the mentoring and encouragement provided by Robert Reed, author of *Indiana's Covered Bridges*. I would like to thank Jenny Capper, my administrative assistant, who aided me in proofreading and editing the manuscript.

I am indebted to the Ohio Historic Bridge Association (OHBA) and its predecessor organizations for their continuing efforts to research, promote, maintain, and restore the covered bridges in Ohio. Its Web site at www.oldohiobridges.com/ohba provided verification of information. The president of OHBA, David Simmons, imparted answers to many questions. The following county engineers made details available about the renovation and restoration of their covered bridges: Stevan Hook (Morgan County), John Smolen (retired, Ashtabula County), Steve Simmons (Preble County), Steve Stolte (retired, Union County), and Jeff Stauch (Union County).

Research included a number of reference works: *Covered Bridges of the Middle West* by Richard Allen; *Covered Bridges on the Byways of Ohio* by Bryon Ketcham; *Covered Bridges of Fairfield County* by John Klages; *World Guide to Covered Bridges* by Oscar Lane, editor; *Ohio Historic Bridge Guide* by the Ohio Historic Bridge Association; *Indiana's Covered Bridges* by Robert Reed; *Covered Wooden Truss Bridges of Green County, Ohio* by James Shell; *Muskingum River Covered Bridges* by Norris Schneider; *Stagecoach Inns, Hotels, Covered Bridges, and Towns in Wyandot County* by Arethusa Watts; *The Covered Bridges of Ohio* by Miriam Wood; *Covered Bridges: Ohio, Kentucky, and West Virginia* by Miriam Wood and David Simmons.

The postcards illustrated in this book are from the author's private collection.

INTRODUCTION

The author's interest in covered bridges was spurred by stories told by her mother, Daisy, who played in the rippling waters beneath the Island Run Covered Bridge (Helmick Mill) early in the 20th century. Interlaced with accounts of the hardships of rural life were tales carried down from Grandfather Morris about Morgan's Raiders. Gen. John Hunt Morgan and his Confederate raiders forayed through southern Ohio in 1863, wreaking havoc, destroying property, and burning covered bridges. They were pursed by the Union Army as well as state militia. As a small band of the raiders approached Island Run, they were captured by Morgan County militiamen. The captives were held overnight in Helmick Mill, where one of the prisoners managed to escape. The captives were then transferred to Columbus, where General Morgan and the remainder of his cavalry had been moved after capture in Columbiana County. Residents of Morgan County were fortunate that their mill and nearby property had not burned or been damaged. The government paid out over $576,000 to 4,400 Ohioans filing claims for damages.

Island Run Covered Bridge is 1 of 142 historic covered bridges existing in Ohio. The countryside around the bridge does not look much different than it did in 1867. It has recently been restored, but the area nearby is very isolated in a deep "hollar." Located on a dirt and gravel covered road, the bridge is one of the most picturesque in Ohio. Water cascades over rocky crags and outcrops below, creating an enchanting waterfall. The surrounding area is a beautiful spot to take a picnic lunch and spend the afternoon wading and stepping from rock to rock through the stony bottom of the run.

When Ohio was admitted to the Union in 1803, there were no covered bridges in the state. Lush forests blanketed the countryside; creeks and rivers were abundant. The Ohio River (Algonquin for "beautiful") forms the state's southern border and flows from Pittsburgh to the Mississippi River. Because of Ohio's numerous waterways, bridges became a necessity for commerce and travel in the early settlement of the state.

The earliest report of a covered bridge in Ohio was described in the *Navigator* in 1814. Zadock Cramer, seeing a bridge on the mouth of the Little Beaver Creek on the Ohio-Pennsylvania border, described, "At the upper grist mill near the mouth of the creek, is a handsome arched bridge, substantially made and well-covered in, adding great facility to emigrants and travelers passing into the State of Ohio from this Quarter."

Other bridges were soon to follow as pioneers rushed to head west in the settlement of the new land. At one time, Ohio had the distinction of having over 4,000 of the 12,000 estimated covered bridges in the United States—more than any other state. The 142 remaining historical covered bridges make Ohio second to Pennsylvania, which has 219 bridges.

Why were the bridges covered and sided? Romantics imagine the bridges providing cover for trysts of Victorian lovers, as popularized in verses such as, "Kiss your girl when you go through. A short peck'll do for a short bridge, but if it's long and dark there's time enough for a hug 'n' squeeze." Children were enchanted by their whimsy with verses such as, "Make a wish and hold your breath / As we go through. / If you can hold it all the way / Your wish will come true."

The more practical assume the roof and siding of a bridge kept horses pulling their loads across a bridge from shying away from rampaging waters below. While these notions are intriguing, the roof and siding were actually added to provide protection for the framework from the harsh elements of Ohio rain, sleet, ice, and snow. Wood, if protected, can survive 70 to 80 years beyond the lifespan of an uncovered bridge. The availability of plentiful timber in Ohio's abundant forests made these bridges inexpensive and quick to build with resources at hand. It would take six men five or six weeks to complete a 60-foot span by working 10-hour days, five and a half days per week.

Aside from covering the wooden bridge, the most important decision in the building was the truss design. The truss is a series of interlocking triangles providing support and absorbing the stress of the vehicles passing over the bridge. Miriam Wood's *The Covered Bridges of Ohio* provides illustrations and an overview of the various designs used in the construction of Ohio bridges.

What designates a covered bridge as historic? David Simmons, president of the Ohio Historic Bridge Association, explains the historic covered bridge as "any covered bridge built before 1919." Timber was used extensively in World War I, and the scarcity and high price of lumber made it too expensive to build or replace wooden bridges. New and replacement bridges were therefore built of other less expensive and more abundant materials. Other covered bridges became extinct because they were unable to carry the heavier and wider loads required for an emerging commerce. Many remaining covered bridges floated away in floods (such as the great flood of 1913), collapsed because of heavy loads, fell to arson, were demolished, or deteriorated in abject abandonment.

Many of the vintage postcards collected by the author had a series of handwritten numbers on the reverse side. These numbers were a cataloguing system designed by John Diehl to identify covered bridges in the United States. The first number was assigned to each state corresponding to an alphabetical listing of the states. Ohio became 33, and later 35 as more states were added to the Union. Alphabetically, a second number was assigned for each of Ohio's 88 counties. The final classification was the record of the bridge in the specific county. Thus, the Island Run Covered Bridge in Morgan County, Ohio, is classified as 35-58-35.

This book captures in vintage postcards the images of more than 200 historical Ohio covered bridges, both bygone and surviving. The GPS location is listed for existing bridges. For some covered bridges, the image on a postcard is all that remains; others, never photographed or depicted, are lost forever.

One

ADAMS COUNTY THROUGH FAIRFIELD COUNTY

ADAMS COUNTY, GOVERNOR KIRKER COVERED BRIDGE (35-01-10). Built askew in 1890 over the east fork of Eagle Creek, the bridge bears the name of Thomas Kirker, who became interim governor of Ohio in 1807. The Kirker farm, a cemetery, and a bicentennial barn are located near the single-span, 63-foot, multiple kingpost truss (MKP) bridge. In 1950, the bridge was reinforced with steel beams and rods. (GPS: N38 47.05 W 83 36.21)

ADAMS COUNTY, HARSHAVILLE COVERED BRIDGE (35-01-02). In 1863, Gen. John Morgan's Confederate raiders crossed into Ohio, burning bridges to avoid pursuit by Union militiamen. They spared this bridge but ransacked the Harshaville general store, carrying off bolts of calico. The pre–Civil War construction (1855) is a single-span, 110-foot, MKP bridge crossing Grace Run Creek. It is named for the Harsha family, who built a mill there. (GPS: N38 54.35 W83 33.18)

ASHLAND COUNTY, ROCHESTER MILL COVERED BRIDGE (35-03-02). The bridge is surrounded by debris from the great flood of 1913. The flood, which swept over Ohio in late March, destroyed many covered bridges and spelled the end of their heyday. This single-span bridge stood over Lake Fork of the Mohican River. Built in 1870, it was the last bridge in Ashland County.

Rochester Mill   Ashland County, Ohio   35-03-02R

ASHTABULA COUNTY, BLAINE ROAD COVERED BRIDGE (35-04-02). This 112-foot bridge, built in 1862 of Town truss design, burned down in July 1962. It was nestled in the hollow at the bottom of a long, curving hill and crossed the Ashtabula River in a single span. Ashtabula County has the most covered bridges in Ohio with 17; of those, 12 are historic.

Dewey Road   Ashtabula County, Ohio   35-04-03

ASHTABULA COUNTY, DEWEY ROAD OR OLIN BRIDGE (35-04-03). Mr. Potter built this 115-foot, Town truss bridge in 1873 to span the Ashtabula River. Ashtabula County engineer John Smolen convinced county officials to restore historic bridges and build new ones as tourist attractions. Under Smolen's master plan, this span was restored in 1984 and rebuilt in 1994. (GPS: N41 51.76 W80 43.26)

ASHTABULA COUNTY, CREEK ROAD COVERED BRIDGE (35-04-05). The 112-foot, Town truss design is one of two bridges crossing the Conneaut River. Built in 1880, it was repaired in 1963, giving it a new look; it was restored in 1996. The Conneaut River comes from Pennsylvania and meanders through this area of Ohio before veering north to Lake Erie. (GPS: N41 55.18 W80 36.57)

ASHTABULA COUNTY, MIDDLE ROAD COVERED BRIDGE (35-04-06). Built in 1868, this 136-foot, Howe truss bridge also spans the Conneaut River. In 1984, a broken timber caused it to sag dangerously. John Smolen garnered a crew of volunteers to save the bridge and make extensive repairs. Maintaining and building bridges is no easy task in Ashtabula County, which has record snowfalls each year. (GPS: N41 54.11 W80 32.83)

ASHTABULA COUNTY, FURNACE ROAD COVERED BRIDGE (35-04-07). This bridge, built in 1868, once spanned Conneaut Creek. The 134-foot, Howe truss span stood until 1950, when the road was relocated.

ASHTABULA COUNTY, KELLOGSVILLE COVERED BRIDGE (35-04-08). The 70-foot, Town truss bridge over the Ashtabula River was removed in 1947. The majority of covered bridges in Ashtabula County were of Town truss (lattice) design. Ithiel Town of Connecticut patented his wood truss design in 1820.

ASHTABULA COUNTY, ROOT ROAD COVERED BRIDGE (35-04-09). The bridge crosses a branch of the Ashtabula River. The 97-foot, Town truss span was built in 1868 and restored in 1982–1983. Ithiel Town's agents charged a royalty of $1 per foot to those using his design. (GPS: N41 49.99 W80 37.22)

ASHTABULA COUNTY, HILDOM ROAD COVERED BRIDGE (35-04-10). Melting snow on the banks and in the creek below paints a bleak image of this vanished bridge. The single-span, 75-foot bridge crossed the Ashtabula Creek and was replaced by a new steel bridge in 1955.

ASHTABULA COUNTY, ADAMS ROAD COVERED BRIDGE (35-04-11). The lattice-type, single-span, 103-foot bridge crossed the Ashtabula River. The postcard depicts the south end in 1947 before it was removed. The word *Ashtabula* means "fish river." Modern farming has nearly dried up the once-thriving river where fishing was abundant.

ASHTABULA COUNTY, BENETKA ROAD COVERED BRIDGE (35-04-12). Built over the Ashtabula River, the bridge is a 115-foot, Town lattice design. Although it is listed as being built in 1900, it is thought to be much older. An arch was added during renovation in 1985. (GPS: N41 50.91 W80 41.36)

15

ASHTABULA COUNTY, GRAHAM ROAD COVERED BRIDGE (35-04-13). The 85-foot bridge, built in 1867, once spanned the Ashtabula River. Of Town truss design, it was closed to motor traffic and moved off the creek to a small rural park in 1972. (GPS: N41 46.88 W80 37.09)

ASHTABULA COUNTY, SOUTH DENMARK BRIDGE (35-04-14). Built in 1868, the 80-foot, single-span, Town truss bridge crosses Mill Creek, a branch of the Grand River. It was bypassed in 1975, and reopened in 1984. (GPS: N41 43.02 W80 41.42)

ASHTABULA COUNTY, MARCH ROAD COVERED BRIDGE (35-04-15). The 108-foot, lattice-type bridge spanned Mill Creek east of Jefferson, Ohio. It was built in 1862 and abandoned when the road changed. Sun is seen shining through the lattice where the siding has fallen away.

ASHTABULA COUNTY, DOYLE ROAD OR MULLEN COVERED BRIDGE (35-04-16). The sturdy, 84-foot, old Town lattice span (1868) over Mill Creek makes a pleasing overlook to a still pond below. Doyle Road makes a square turn at each end, and short windows were installed in order to see approaching traffic. An arch was added during rehabilitation in 1988. (GPS: N41 45.72 W80. 47.42)

ASHTABULA COUNTY, EAGLEVILLE OR FOREMAN ROAD COVERED BRIDGE (35-04-17). This winter scene is reflected beautifully in the water of Mill Creek. The 135-foot, Town truss bridge was built in 1862. Eagleville was so named because eagles habitually perched at a nearby mill. In 1972, the bridge was sold for $5 to the present owner, who incorporated the truss timbers into the interior design of a pizza parlor in Kingsville.

ASHTABULA COUNTY, MECHANICSVILLE COVERED BRIDGE (35-04-18). Built in 1867, this single-span, 154-foot, Howe truss bridge of wood and iron has an arch 28 inches thick. It is the oldest of the county's bridges. Renovated in 2003 by engineer Tim Martin, it was opened to traffic in 2004. An antique hayfork is now mounted on each gable. (GPS: N41 45.26 W80 53.88)

ASHTABULA COUNTY, HARPERSFIELD BRIDGE (35-04-19). The refreshing scene is reminiscent of days gone by. There was once a mill, and later (1901) a waterworks generated electricity. Windows were cut for visibility because of hazardous curves at the north end. Built by Mr. Potter in 1868, it is Ohio's longest historic covered bridge at 234 feet. Originally it was a two-span, Howe Truss type, crossing the Grand River at old State Route 534. The 1913 flood cut a new channel around the end of the bridge, and a third steel span was added. John Smolen restored the bridge in 1992. The 613-foot-long, Smolen-Gulf Covered Bridge (page 124), built in 2008, is the longest covered bridge in the United States, with four spans standing 93 feet above the Ashtabula River. It cost $8 million to build. (GPS: N41 45.33 W80 56.68)

ASHTABULA COUNTY, EAST TRUMBULL COVERED BRIDGE (35-04-20). This bridge on Windsor-Mechanicsville Road spanned Trumbull Creek east of Trumbull. The 100-foot single span was replaced by a new type of bridge in 1950.

ASHTABULA COUNTY, SHAUNGHUM (FOBES ROAD) COVERED BRIDGE (35-04-21). This 125-foot, Howe truss bridge stood high over Grand River on Fobes Road. A shelter panel added 11 feet to its length, and it had the appearance of standing on stilts. By 1971, it had deteriorated, and it was listing on its "stilts" and in danger of collapse when the county asked the fire department to burn it as a fire exercise.

ASHTABULA COUNTY, RIVERDALE COVERED BRIDGE (35-04-22). Built in 1874, the 120-foot, Town truss bridge spans the Grand River west of Rock Creek. It was restored in 1981. The Grand River has been reduced to a stream since forest areas have been cleared. (GPS: N41 40.39 W80 52.32)

ASHTABULA COUNTY, ROCK CREEK COVERED BRIDGE (35-04-23). Built in 1832, this 114-foot, Town truss bridge was of wooden-peg construction. The double-barreled (two lanes) span crossed Rock Creek. The bridge was constructed by Ackley and Crowell Builders for the Trumbull and Ashtabula Turnpike Company. A steel span replaced it in 1948.

ASHTABULA COUNTY, WARNER'S HOLLOW/WINDSOR MILL COVERED BRIDGE (35-04-25). This bridge, like many where there were mills, spans a deep, picturesque gorge over Phelps Creek near Windsor, Ohio. The 120-foot span was originally built in 1835 and rebuilt in 1867; it was renovated in 2002–2004. A typical sign often found on covered bridges read, "Walk Your Horse or Pay a Fine." The picturesque scene shows the bridge from below. The Town truss design is supported by abutments and piers of fieldstone and sandstone that came from quarries that once flourished in the Windsor area. (GPS: N41 31.98 W80 57.84)

ASHTABULA COUNTY, CALLENDAR BRIDGE (35-04-24). Winter wields the artist's brush to create this scene of quiet beauty. The three-span, 73-foot, Town truss bridge, built in the 1900s to replace an earlier crossing (1860), stood over Rock Creek until 1966, when a development company bought it for $1. When it was discovered that the cost to relocate it would be $11,000, it was burned instead.

ASHTABULA COUNTY, SOUTH WINDSOR ROAD COVERED BRIDGE (35-04-26). Built in 1870, the single-span, 87-foot bridge spanned the Grand River. Windsor Road was once known as Old Plank Road, so named because the original road between Warren and Painesville was made of wooden planks, which eventually rotted out and sank into a bog.

ATHENS COUNTY, PALOS OR NEWTON COVERED BRIDGE (35-05-01). The 75-foot, MKP bridge, built in 1875, crosses Sunday Creek. In 1977, the bridge was boarded up on the inside to keep vandals from stealing the siding and to prevent the accumulation of trash along the lower chords. Three covered bridges still stand in this once thriving coal-mining county, which derived its name from Athens, Greece. (GPS: N39 31.51 W82 04.30)

ATHENS COUNTY, KIDWELL COVERED BRIDGE (35-05-02). Also spanning Sunday Creek, at 96 feet, this is the longest of the three bridges in Athens County. The Howe truss design was built by the Hocking Valley Bridge Works of Lancaster in 1880. It was closed in 1978, when an overloaded truck caused extensive damage. Items posted on the bridge are reminiscent of advertising once plastered on bridges. (GPS: 39 27.34 W82 06.19)

ATHENS COUNTY, BLACKWOOD/PRATTS FORK COVERED BRIDGE (35-05-06). This 64-foot bridge spans the Middle Branch of Shade River. Of MKP design, it was built in 1881 by E. B. Henderson. Steel tension rods were added in 1905 to strengthen the old trusses; a steel pier was placed for support in 1975. It was named for the Blackwood family, who owned a large portion of the township. (GPS: N39 11.83 W81 58.46)

BROWN COUNTY, NEW HOPE OR BETHEL ROAD COVERED BRIDGE (35-08-05). The bridge is the longest (170 feet) single-span covered bridge in Ohio. Jacob Bower, who constructed numerous bridges in Brown County with his sons, built the Howe truss span in 1878 over White Oak Creek. One son was killed while building a bridge. Another son rebuilt this bridge in 1932, as well as a grandson in 1977. (GPS: N38 57.57 W83 54.94)

BROWN COUNTY, McCAFFERTY COVERED BRIDGE (35-08-08). Built by the Smith Bridge Company in 1870, the 157-foot, Howe truss bridge spans the east fork of the Little Miami River. William Howe's truss design (1840) used iron rods as truss tension members. It could be assembled rapidly and the tension easily adjusted. (GPS: N39 09.09 W83 59.65)

BROWN COUNTY, JAMESON COVERED BRIDGE (35-08-11). Built in the 1870s, this bridge spanned Straight Creek. The 136-foot structure was named for the owner of a stone house nearby. It was 1 of 80 covered bridges built in Brown County; only 6 remain.

BROWN COUNTY, COLUMBUS-YOUNG COVERED BRIDGE (35-08-12). The span crossed White Oak Creek halfway between Georgetown and Higginsport on the Ohio River. Erected in 1873 by the Toledo Bridge Company, it was factory built, shipped, and reassembled on-site. In a ruckus during the construction, a worker carved on a beam, "Hell in the Cabin."

BROWN COUNTY, EAGLE CREEK COVERED BRIDGE (35-08-18). Sometimes called Bowman Bridge because it was located near Bowman's grocery store, this bridge was built in 1872. The 174-foot, Smith truss span was the last covered bridge in Ohio on a state route—763. It washed away in a flood in 1997.

BROWN COUNTY, SCOFIELD COVERED BRIDGE (35-08-21). This bridge was built in 1875 by local contractor John Griffith and was named for a store and blacksmith shop that stood nearby. It spanned Beetle Creek (the east fork of Eagle Creek) near Ripley and was removed in 1990.

BROWN COUNTY, NORTH POLE ROAD COVERED BRIDGE (35-08-23). The 156-foot, Smith truss bridge was built in 1875 over Eagle Creek near Ripley. At one time a sign on the bridge warned not to carry fire over the bridge. Burning was a real danger for wooden covered bridges. The floods of 1997 heavily damaged the span. (GPS: N38 45.00 W83 46.39)

BROWN COUNTY, GEORGE MILLER COVERED BRIDGE (35-08-34). Built in 1878, the 154-foot, Smith truss bridge spans Eagle Creek near Russelville. (GPS: N38 50.24 W83 45.04)

BUTLER COUNTY, BLACK OR PUGH'S MILL COVERED BRIDGE (35-09-03). Before 1860, all bridges in Butler County were toll bridges. In 1868, Black Bridge (earlier called Oxford Bridge) was the first bridge to be built by the county. As a result of remodeling work done in 1869, the 206-foot, two-span bridge is a combination of both Childs and Long trusses. (GPS: N39 31.42 W84 44.10)

CLARK COUNTY, SPRINGFIELD COVERED BRIDGE (35-12-?). Pictured is Springfield in 1850 looking south. The two-lane bridge spanned Buck Creek. Barrett's Mill can be seen to the left of the bridge and a women's seminary just north of it. At least 17 covered bridges were on the National Road between Zanesville and the Indiana line. Four were in Clark County, spanning Buck Creek and Mad River. Springfield is home to Wittenberg University.

CLERMONT COUNTY, PERINTOWN OR STONELICK COVERED BRIDGE (35-13-02). The Howe truss, 140-foot bridge, constructed in 1878, is the only surviving bridge of the two that once spanned Stonelick Creek. It has been damaged several times by trucks carrying heavy loads. (GPS: N39 07.88 W84 11.21)

CLINTON COUNTY, MARTINSVILLE COVERED BRIDGE (35-14-09). Built in 1871, the MKP, 72-foot bridge, spanning Todds Fork, is the last in Clinton County. It is the oldest existing bridge constructed by Champion Bridge Company. Renovations were made in the 1970s, which included steel beams and new concrete abutments. (GPS: N39 19.78 W83 50.09)

COLUMBIANA COUNTY, McCLELLAN OR KINMUER COVERED BRIDGE (35-15-02). A mantle of ermine surrounds this winter scene of the bridge built over west fork of Little Beaver Creek in 1871. The MKP, 53-foot span is closed to motor traffic. At one time, Columbiana County had over 240 covered bridges. (GPS: N40 43.73 W80 50.13)

COLUMBIANA COUNTY, SELLS OR ROLLER MILL COVERED BRIDGE (35-15-01). Over 100 short covered bridges like Sells Bridge once spanned Little Beaver Creek and its tributaries. Built in 1878, the 50-foot bridge was removed from its original location in 1992 and dismantled. In 1994, it was rebuilt in Scenic Vista Park south of Lisbon. Confederate general John Morgan was captured in Columbiana County in 1863. Morgan burned no bridges in this county. (GPS: N40 44.30 W 80 49.18)

COLUMBIANA COUNTY, MCKAIG'S COVERED BRIDGE (35-15-03). The bridge, which spanned Little Beaver Creek, was destroyed by arson in June 1988. The images of the children playing here are only a memory. A broken millstone and the remains of an old earthen dam mutely testify to a days of greater glory.

COLUMBIANA COUNTY, MILLER ROAD COVERED BRIDGE (35-15-07). Unroofed by a tornado in 1959, this little snow-covered bridge spanned Mill Seat Creek. The 37-foot span built in 1860 survived that disaster, only to be burned by an arsonist in 1995.

COLUMBIANA COUNTY, TEEGARDEN OR CENTENNIAL COVERED BRIDGE (35-15-05). An almost perfect image of the bridge is reflected in the water below. Better known as the Centennial Bridge, it was built in 1876, just 100 years after the Declaration of Independence was signed. Of MKP construction, it spans Little Beaver Creek at 66 feet near an old millrace and pond. It was named after a Mr. U. Teegarden, who owned a tract of land near the bridge. Coal and iron mines typical of the county's industry were located just south of the bridge. It was restored in 2003. (GPS: N40 49.30 W80 49.62)

COLUMBIANA COUNTY, CHURCH HILL ROAD COVERED BRIDGE (35-15-08). Boasted as the shortest covered bridge in the United States, it spans just 22 feet. It was built in 1870 over Middle Fork of Little Beaver Creek. In 1963, when the road was bypassed, the bridge was moved and rebuilt at Elkton near Lock 24 of Sandy and Beaver Canal. (GPS: N40 45.68 W80 42.24)

COLUMBIANA COUNTY, GASTON'S MILL COVERED BRIDGE (35-15-19). The postcard made from a painting owned by Mrs. Harry Warrick is all that remains of this picturesque bridge that once spanned Middle Fork of Little Beaver Creek. It was replaced by an iron bridge.

COLUMBIANA COUNTY, CANTON WOODEN COVERED BRIDGE (35-15-53). Built in 1863, the bridge was located at Walnut Street in Lisbon and spanned Middle Fork of Little Beaver Creek. According to the caption on the back, the postcard was made from a painting completed by Harrison in 1883. The men on the tracks were listed as Jack Starr and Frank Miller.

COLUMBIANA COUNTY, GAS TAX ROAD COVERED BRIDGE (35-15-67). Two women sit beside the deteriorating bridge over the west fork of Little Beaver Creek at Gas Tax Road. The name Columbiana County was derived from the combination of the names of Christopher Columbus and Queen Anne.

COLUMBIANA COUNTY, THOMAS MALONE OR ELKTON COVERED BRIDGE (35-15-96). Thrice moved, the 42-foot span was built in 1870 over Middle Run. About 1900, it was moved to the Wade Huffman farm. In 1912, it was moved to township land and rebuilt for storage. Tom Malone mounted a campaign in the 1970s to move it to Beaver Creek Park, where it was rebuilt over a canal bed. (GPS: N40 43.67 W80 36.72)

COSHOCTON COUNTY, DOUGHTY CREEK COVERED BRIDGE (35-16-01). This 85-foot bridge was built in 1867 for $690. It spanned Doughty Creek at Power's Mill and led into a farmer's field. A flood in July 1969 ripped it off its foundations and deposited it lengthwise into the creek, where water rushed through it. The span was removed from the creek and dismantled. Coshocton County had over 90 wooden truss bridges like this one; only 1 remains.

COSHOCTON COUNTY, HELMICK COVERED BRIDGE (35-16-02). Eli Fox built a mill on this site at Killbuck Creek in 1829. In 1863, John Shrake built this two-span, 166-foot, Buckingham truss bridge. However, the foundation work bears the name of F. Victor, who most likely was the subcontractor. Later a store and post office were erected nearby. The bridge deteriorated in the 1980s but was rebuilt in 1995 and opened to light traffic. (GPS: N40 23.60 W81 56.56)

COSHOCTON COUNTY, OLD CONESVILLE COVERED BRIDGE (35-16-06). The bridge, built in 1875, spanned the Muskingum River between Coshocton and Zanesville. At one time, it was the second-longest covered bridge in the United States at 400 feet. The four-span, Smith truss design cost $7,110 to build. In 1955, it was closed and stood abandoned until 1958, when a contractor poured 150 gallons of gasoline over it and set it on fire.

Wills Creek   Coshocton County, Ohio   35-16-07

COSHOCTON COUNTY, WILLS CREEK OR SANDLES/HAMILTON FARM COVERED BRIDGE (35-16-07). Several bridges were erected to span Wills Creek, like this 137-foot crossing built in 1879. The superstructure cost $1,188, and the foundation cost $1,578. A flood tore out some of its supports during the 1950s. It was used for storage until its demise in 1991, when it fell into the creek. It was one of the last two Burr truss bridges in Ohio.

Walhonding   Coshocton County, Ohio   35-16-16   67-88

COSHOCTON COUNTY, WALHONDING COVERED BRIDGE (35-16-16). This was the third covered bridge to be built on this site over the Walhonding River. The three-span, 340-foot bridge was constructed by the Smith Bridge Company in 1877 and was destroyed by the 1913 flood.

DELAWARE COUNTY, CHAMBERS ROAD COVERED BRIDGE (35-21-04). This is the only existing covered bridge of the 64 once built in Delaware County. Spanning Big Walnut Creek, the 73-foot, Childs truss bridge was constructed by Everett Sherman in 1883. This is the only bridge Sherman built outside of Preble County. (GPS: N40 20.23 W82 49.06)

Blacklick   Fairfield County, Ohio   35-23-01

FAIRFIELD COUNTY, BLACKLICK COVERED BRIDGE (35-23-01). Built in 1888 to replace a 56-year-old structure, this 13-panel, Howe truss design spanned Blacklick Creek. The builder was August Borneman, who founded the Hocking Valley Bridge Works. The 133-foot span met its fate in 1977, when a truck carrying 17 tons of gravel attempted to cross, causing its collapse. It was so named because of an outcropping of black shale along its banks.

FAIRFIELD COUNTY, FULTZ COVERED BRIDGE (35-23-05). A favorite in Fairfield County, this bridge crossed Poplar Creek. Built in 1891, it was a 74-foot, MKP design. Its most unusual feature was that it was built askew. The floor was a parallelogram, not the usual rectangle. An arsonist burned it in 1971.

FAIRFIELD COUNTY, SNYDER (SNIDER) NO. 2 COVERED BRIDGE (35-23-06). This span, built in 1888, lost its identity in a column of smoke in July 1965. Snyder No. 1 Bridge, just upstream on Poplar Creek, was removed in 1940.

FAIRFIELD COUNTY, HIZEY OR VISINTINE COVERED BRIDGE (35-23-07). Built by J. W. Buchanan in 1891, the 83-foot, MKP variant originally spanned Poplar Creek. It was named for T. Hizey, owner of the land nearby. In 1986, it was moved to Sycamore Creek on private property and rebuilt in 1989. Well-known watercolorist Leland McClelland painted the bridge and distributed 500 editions of his work. (GPS: N39 54.88 W82 42.57)

FAIRFIELD COUNTY, MACKLIN HOUSE OR TUSSING HILL COVERED BRIDGE (35-23-08). Built in 1880, this bridge had a peaceful setting among the large sycamores shading Poplar Creek. The 65-foot, Burr arch structure was damaged in the 1913 flood and rebuilt by J. W. Buchanan in 1916. It was demolished in 1971.

FAIRFIELD COUNTY, JON BRIGHT NO. 2 COVERED BRIDGE (35-23-10). Combining both wood and metal construction, the 75-foot span was built in 1881 across Poplar Creek. It has a bowstring suspension in combination with an inverted arch—one of two remaining in Ohio. A church and camp meeting grounds were nearby. The bridge was moved to Ohio University's Lancaster campus in 1988. (GPS: N39 44.26 W 82 35.08)

FAIRFIELD COUNTY, GEORGE HUTCHINS COVERED BRIDGE (35-23-13). Built in 1904, the 62-foot, MKP bridge spanned Clear Creek and was part of Zane's Trace, a pioneer trail (see page 60). It was dismantled in 1988 and moved to Alley Park south of Lancaster where it was rebuilt in 2000. (GPS: N39 40.81 W82 34.75)

FAIRFIELD COUNTY, HANNAWAY OR CLEARPORT COVERED BRIDGE (35–23–15). One of two bridges still spanning Clear Creek, this crossing was built in 1881 and rebuilt in 1901. Constructed by James Buchanan, the 86-foot, MKP design replaced an earlier bridge. Fairfield County once had the second-highest number of covered bridges in the nation with 279 documented. (GPS: N39 37.11 W82 40.79)

FAIRFIELD COUNTY, JOHNSON OR TERRY MILL COVERED BRIDGE (35–23–16). The other existing bridge on Clear Creek is gracefully situated in a pleasant environment. Built in 1887 by August Borneman, the 98-foot, Howe truss design is closed to traffic. Terry Mill stood near the bridge in the vicinity of Hopewell Church. It is almost a twin of the Hannaway Bridge. (GPS: N39 36.81 W82 39.56)

FAIRFIELD COUNTY, STATE DAM COVERED BRIDGE (35-23-22). James Buchanan built this bridge in 1893 or 1894 to cross Little Walnut Creek. The span was near a system of locks, which in 1829 carried the Ohio-Erie Canal across the creek. The bridge was named for a dam, which washed away in 1894. It was the county's longest single span at 157 feet. Arson claimed the bridge in 1967.

FAIRFIELD COUNTY, LEONARD OR BASIL COVERED BRIDGE (35-23-26). Located just south of Basil (Baltimore) in the shade of old sycamores, the MKP, 96-foot bridge, built around 1889, spanned Walnut Creek. It was removed by the county in 1967.

FAIRFIELD COUNTY, SWARTZ MILL COVERED BRIDGE (35-23-39). Of Burr arch design, this quaint bridge had a wooden-shingled roof. The 91-foot span was built in 1854 to cross Rush Creek. Its open sides gave it a light and delicate look. A mill, post office, and small store sat nearby. It was removed by the county in 1962.

FAIRFIELD COUNTY, MINK HOLLOW COVERED BRIDGE (35-23-43). The awnings serve as an inviting shelter from rain and sun for travelers. The attractive 51-foot bridge, built in 1887, is a MKP truss crossing Arney Run. Three mills once stood nearby, as did a school, which was converted to a residence. (GPS: N39 38.34 W82 38.97)

FAIRFIELD COUNTY, BURTON COVERED BRIDGE (35-23-47). This bridge vanished from view over the brow of the hill on County Road 176 in 1952, when a flash flood washed out an abutment. It spanned a branch of the Hocking River near Lancaster. As late as 1950, there were 46 covered bridges in the county. Now only 16 bridges remain.

FAIRFIELD COUNTY, ROCK MILL COVERED BRIDGE (35-23-48). Built in 1901, this 37-foot bridge replaced an earlier bridge that spanned the Hocking River. The queen post truss was designed by Jacob "Cap" Brandt and built for $575. The most popular bridge in the county, it is a good example of the "house"—a term used by county officials to describe the covered bridges built after 1890. (GPS: N39 44.96 W82 42.80)

FAIRFIELD COUNTY, ROLEY SCHOOL COVERED BRIDGE (35-23-49). The bridge was moved several times from its original location spanning the Basil Canal. Originally built in 1899 by J. W. Buchanan for $490, the 49-foot crossing was first moved north to span Paw Paw Creek on Roley Road. In 1974, it was moved to its present location at the fairgrounds in Lancaster, where it sits over dry land. (GPS: N39 43.48 W82 36.10)

Smith-Carnes   Fairfield County, Ohio   35-23-51R

FAIRFIELD COUNTY, SMITH-CARNES COVERED BRIDGE (FORMERLY JACKSON-ETY) (35-23-51). This nine-panel, 87-foot, MKP design was built in 1854 over the Ohio Canal in Carroll. Albert Sartain, sheriff of Franklin County, moved the bridge to Walnut Creek by the Smith farm in 1912. The new location gave access to farm fields. It collapsed in 1993.

Two

Fayette County through Muskingum County

Fayette County, Yankeetown Road Covered Bridge (35-24-03). The eye-catching image reflected in the water below is the only trace of this bridge, which was destroyed by arsonists in 1965. Built over Deer Creek in 1877, the 246-foot, Howe truss crossing was once Ohio's longest timber truss. Fayette County once had 66 covered bridges.

FRANKLIN COUNTY, BERGSTRESSER OR DIETZ COVERED BRIDGE (35-25-03). Located near Canal Winchester and spanning Walnut Creek, this is the last covered bridge in the county where 176 once stood. It was built in 1887 by the Columbus Bridge Company for $2,690. In 1991, the 125-foot, Partridge truss span was completely renovated with foundation work and replacement of rotted timbers, a roof, and siding. (GPS: N39 49.81 W82 48.99)

GREENE COUNTY, FEEDWIRE COVERED BRIDGE (FORMERLY 35-29-09) NOW CARILLON PARK COVERED BRIDGE (35-57-03). Built in 1870 by the Smith Bridge Company, the 42-foot Warren truss originally spanned Little Sugar Creek near Bellbrook. In 1948, the bridge was purchased by the National Cash Register Company, dismantled, and moved to its current location at Carillon Park in Dayton. In the rebuilding, it was significantly altered in appearance. (GPS: N39 43.66 W84 12.12.)

Jacoby Road   Greene County, Ohio   35-29-14

GREENE COUNTY, JACOBY ROAD COVERED BRIDGE (35-29-14). This crossing was one of two Wernwag truss bridges constructed by Henry Hebble. Built for $15.55 per linear foot in 1869, the 145-foot span crossed the Little Miami River. It was named for John Jacoby, who owned a mill just north of the bridge. A wooden dam upstream formed a millpond, furnishing water for the mill. It was destroyed by arson in 1970.

GREENE COUNTY, STEVENSON ROAD COVERED BRIDGE (35-29-15). Built by the Smith Bridge Company over Massie's Creek in 1877, the 95-foot, Smith truss span is a pleasure to view on a summer day. It was closed to traffic and bypassed in 2004. (GPS: N39 44.11 W83 53.94)

51

Charleton Mill Road   Greene County, Ohio   35-29-16

GREENE COUNTY, CHARLETON MILL ROAD COVERED BRIDGE (35-29-16). Henry Hebble, who built bridges in Fairfield County, erected this 119-foot span in 1883 over Massie's Creek. Big Stream Mill was built there in 1837 and later renamed. The milldam was half a mile upstream. Nearby is Wilberforce University, the oldest historically black college in the United States, which is named for the English abolitionist William Wilberforce. (GPS: N39 43.76 W83 52.23)

GREENE COUNTY, BALLARD ROAD COVERED BRIDGE (35-29-18). The 80-foot bridge was built in 1883 by J. C. Brown and named for Lyman Ballard, who established a gristmill nearby in the early 1850s. It is a seven-panel, Howe truss span crossing the North Branch of Caesar's Creek. Once in pastoral surroundings, it can be viewed on the north side of new U.S. 35 near Jamestown, Ohio. (GPS: N39 40.68 W83 48.90)

Jasper Road   Greene County, Ohio   35-29-●R 26

GREENE COUNTY, JASPER ROAD COVERED BRIDGE (WAS 35-29-26 NOW 35-57-36). The 50-foot, Warren truss bridge with arch was originally built in 1869 to span Caesar's Creek at Jasper Road. In 1964, the owner of Mud Lick Estates bought the bridge. He completely disassembled it and moved it to its present location in Montgomery County. (GPS: N39 37.03 W84 24.52)

GUERNSEY COUNTY, BIRD'S RUN COVERED BRIDGE (35-30-01). The 49-foot, MKP design crossed Bird's Run Creek and was replaced in 1956. Guernsey County once had 115 covered bridges; only 2 still stand.

53

Indian Camp Run   Guernsey County, Ohio   35-30-04

GUERNSEY COUNTY, INDIAN CAMP COVERED BRIDGE (35-30-04). The 36-foot, MKP structure, built in 1866, has been heavily reinforced with steel beams. It spans Indian Camp Run. It got its name because of the many American Indian camps that were once situated along the stream. The local mailman once extinguished a brushfire igniting the bridge. (GPS: N40 06.775 W81 38.950)

Kennedy   Guernsey County, Ohio   35-30-05R

GUERNSEY COUNTY, KENNEDY COVERED BRIDGE (35-30-05). This 128-foot, MKP bridge stood 22 feet over Willis Creek. Built in 1883, it replaced an earlier covered bridge. In 1953, it was renovated, and a 30-foot span of the bridge was replaced with a steel pony truss. The remaining covered portion was replaced by a steel structure in 1962.

Milligan　　Guernsey County, Ohio　　35-30-03

GUERNSEY COUNTY, MILLIGAN COVERED BRIDGE (35-30-06). The 52-foot structure was built in 1884 by John and Alex Milligan over Sugar Tree Fork. It was the second bridge at that location. Plans were made to relocate the bridge when State Fork Dam was to be filled, but before it could be moved, it was burned by vandals in 1966.

GUERNSEY COUNTY, GUNN COVERED BRIDGE (35-30-10). The 64-foot, MKP bridge was another spanning Sugar Tree Fork. It was left in place when the Salt Fork Valley was flooded. It could be seen partially above water (and was sometimes used as shelter during storms by boaters) until the early 1980s, when it finally collapsed. The abutments, iron support beams, and some flooring could be seen when the water level was low.

55

Leeper　　　Guernsey County, Ohio　　　35-30-08R

GUERNSEY COUNTY, LEEPER COVERED BRIDGE (35-30-08). The horizontal siding on this bridge is unusual, as most bridges have vertical siding. It was built in the 1840s or 1850s across Salt Fork Creek. When Salt Fork Reservoir was to be filled, this bridge was slated to be saved by moving it to a park in Cambridge. In 1964, before it could be moved, an overloaded truck caused its collapse. Many covered bridges in Guernsey County were in the path of the State Fork Dam.

GUERNSEY COUNTY, ARMSTRONG OR CLIO COVERED BRIDGE (35-30-12). Built in 1891 by Abraham Armstrong at his mill in Clio for $510, this is the fourth-oldest covered bridge in Ohio. This was the only covered bridge to be saved when the Salt Creek Reservoir was filled. In 1966, the 76-foot MKP span was moved to Cambridge City Park. (GPS: N40 02.48 W81 35.86)

Armstrong Mill   Cambridge, Ohio   35-30-12M   67-101

Skull Fork   Guernsey County, Ohio   35-30-16   67-92

GUERNSEY COUNTY, SKULL FORK COVERED BRIDGE (35-30-16). The barren, dirt-covered road can be viewed through the portals of this lonely wooden bridge. The span crossed Skull Fork in Londonderry Township southeast of Antrim.

Oxford Twp.   Guernsey County, Ohio   35-30-23   67-99

GUERNSEY COUNTY, OXFORD TOWNSHIP COVERED BRIDGE (35-30-23). A car waits on the other side of this bridge to pick up the lovely ladies on their Sunday afternoon stroll. This bridge crossed Salt Fork north of Quaker City. It was removed in 1934–1935.

Quaker City   Guernsey County, Ohio   35-30-35

GUERNSEY COUNTY, GILDEA OR HAMMOND COVERED BRIDGE (35-30-28, ALSO IDENTIFIED AS 35-30-35). The bridge with a sidewalk was at the center of Quaker City at Leatherwood Creek. Covered bridges often had multiple uses, and this one was the scene of a wedding in 1874. However, in 1885, it was badly damaged by flooding. The span was dismantled and the timbers floated down Leatherwood Creek, where it was rebuilt at a site near Gibson Station. The rebuilt bridge was replaced in 1958. During the Civil War, Morgan's Raiders zigzagged across southern Ohio. Several bridges in Guernsey County, including another bridge over Leatherwood Creek, were burned. The raiders burned their last bridge at Nebo in Jefferson County before being captured near West Point. A crossing burned by the raiders and later rebuilt was known as "Morgan's Burnt Bridge."

Webster   Guernsey County, Ohio   35-30-29

GUERNSEY COUNTY, WEBSTER COVERED BRIDGE (35-30-29). Built over Leatherwood Creek near Salesville in 1894, this bridge was washed out by a flood in 1946. It was reported to have a Howe truss and was built by Coultas and Lovell Bridge Builders.

Wills Creek and Old Double Bridge, Cambridge, Ohio

GUERNSEY COUNTY, OLD NATIONAL ROAD OR CAMBRIDGE COVERED BRIDGE (35-30-31). Zane's Trace, the first pioneer passage through Ohio, was nothing more than a blazed trail. In 1796–1797, undergrowth and trees were removed, and the trace was completed between Wheeling and Limestone, Kentucky. From 1798 to 1805, pioneers traveling west used a ferry at Zane's Trace Crossing. From 1805 until 1828, when the covered bridge was completed, travelers crossed on a log span.

Old National   Guernsey County, Ohio   35-30-31

GUERNSEY COUNTY, OLD NATIONAL ROAD OR CAMBRIDGE COVERED BRIDGE (35-30-31). The National Road (authorized by Congress in 1806) crossed this covered bridge at Cambridge City and then headed through Guernsey County. Although authorized in 1801, the Old National Road Bridge was not constructed until 1828. Designed by Lewis Wernwag and built by J. P. Shannon, the span was the first bridge in Guernsey County. It was constructed on dry ground and the water turned to flow under it. Wernwag used Ithiel Town's patented lattice truss. The double-lane structure remained in use until it was badly damaged by the 1913 flood and was removed.

The Old Bridge on National Pike, Cambridge, Ohio.

Frisbee Farm   Guernsey County, Ohio   35-30-32

GUERNSEY COUNTY, FRISBEE FARM COVERED BRIDGE (35-30-32). This private bridge over Buffalo Creek is believed to have been built about 1861 by William Crow. Of single king post construction, it was more than 40 feet long. Abutments and a pier of concrete blocks were added later.

Reservoir   Guernsey County, Ohio   35-30-33

GUERNSEY COUNTY, B&O'S RESERVOIR COVERED BRIDGE (35-30-33). The B&O Railroad built this 45-foot bridge in 1901 to provide access to build the reservoir for the locomotives' water supply. Of MKP design, it spanned Leatherwood Creek. After decades of disuse and neglect, it collapsed in 1993.

Red   Guernsey County, Ohio   35-30-34   67-100

GUERNSEY COUNTY, RED COVERED BRIDGE (35-30-34). This bridge crossed Leatherwood Creek on the old portion of the Quaker City-Batesville Road. One of the few bridges with a slate roof, it was removed shortly after 1956.

Winterset   Guernsey County, Ohio   35-30-48   67-98

GUERNSEY COUNTY, WINTERSET OR BRUSHY CREEK COVERED BRIDGE (35-30-48). This bridge was located 100 yards from the George Stewart Store in Winterset. The span crossed Brushy Fork. It was removed sometime after 1934.

HAMILTON COUNTY, JEDIAH HILL OR GROFF MILL COVERED BRIDGE (35-31-01). This two-span, 44-foot, queen post (QP) bridge, which crosses a branch of Mill Creek, was built in 1850. When it partially collapsed in the 1950s, extensive repairs were made. By the 1980s, it could not carry the load of emergency vehicles, so a new concrete and steel substructure was built in 1981. (GPS: N39 15.12 W84 32.69)

HARRISON COUNTY, SKULL FORK COVERED BRIDGE (35-34-19). The county's last covered bridge stands near Freeport. The single-span, 45-foot, MKP crossing was bypassed by the road in the 1970s. Its metal roof was replaced with wood shingles during an earlier renovation, and it was restored in 2008. (GPS: N40 10.97 W81 16.02)

Brushy Fork Harrison County, Ohio 35-34-28

HARRISON COUNTY, BRUSHY FORK COVERED BRIDGE (35-34-28). This bridge was in Cadiz Township. It was framed like a barn with a door and could be classified as stringer construction.

BRIDGE #101 LAUREL CR. WASHINGTON TWP.
HARRISON CO. TIPPECANOE, OHIO.

HARRISON COUNTY, UNKNOWN NAME. (35-34-?). This is one of the three bridges that spanned Laurel Creek. There were once 53 covered bridges in Harrison County. Their dates were not well recorded.

HIGHLAND COUNTY, BARRETT MILL COVERED BRIDGE (35-36-11). Rocky Fork Creek winds through the county passing by where Barrett Mill and Covered Bridge once stood. The span was built around 1870 as a 156-foot Long truss. This beauty was destroyed by an arsonist in 1980.

JACKSON COUNTY, JOHNSON ROAD OR CRABTREE OR PETERSBURG COVERED BRIDGE (35-40-06). This is the last survivor of the three Smith truss bridges that once spanned the Little Scioto River. The 71-foot single span was built in 1870. Jackson County once had 32 covered bridges. (GPS: N38 57.52 W82 47.26)

JACKSON COUNTY, BYER COVERED BRIDGE (35-40-08). Built in 1872, the 74-foot span crosses Pigeon Creek and, like other bridges in Jackson County, is a Smith truss design. Robert Smith of Tipp City patented his truss in 1867. It featured braces set at 45 degrees and counter braces set at 60 degrees. The bridge was restored in 2003. (GPS: N39 10.77 W82 37.88)

JACKSON COUNTY, BUCKEYE FURNACE COVERED BRIDGE (35-40-11). Built in 1871 and located in eastern Jackson County, the 59-foot, Smith truss bridge spans Little Raccoon Creek. The Buckeye Furnace State Memorial is nearby. The area is famous for smelting iron ore. (GPS: N39 03.27 W82 27.58)

LAKE COUNTY, BLAIR COVERED BRIDGE (35-43-01). The 150-foot, Howe truss bridge over the Grand River lasted from 1866 until 1951, when it was replaced by a cement bridge. It was the last remaining bridge in Lake County. Terrain in this area is rugged, and massive cliffs are near where the bridge stood.

LAKE COUNTY, PAINESVILLE COVERED BRIDGE (35-43-?). Lake County is on Lake Erie between Cuyahoga and Ashtabula Counties. There were only 11 covered bridges in this county. Not much is known about this bridge formerly East of Painesville on what is now U.S. 20.

LAWRENCE COUNTY, FOX HOLLOW COVERED BRIDGE (35-44-02). Lawrence County is located along the Ohio River in the heart of the Hanging Rock Iron Region, which produced much of the iron used for armament during the Civil War. There were once 80 covered bridges in the county. William Hosey built this Long truss bridge in 1880, and it was removed in 1967.

Bennington Twp.   Licking County, Ohio   35-45-01

LICKING COUNTY, BELLE HALL COVERED BRIDGE (35-45-01). The 56-foot, MKP truss bridge was built in 1879 to span Otter Fork of the Licking River. The bridge sank into decrepit condition after being damaged by an overloaded truck in the early 1970s. Although rehabilitated with steel chords in 1973, it collapsed under heavy snow cover in 1999.

LICKING COUNTY, BOY SCOUT CAMP OR RAINROCK COVERED BRIDGE (35-45-04). This bridge was relocated from Eden-Mary Township to the Boy Scout Camp in 1974. The 49-foot, MKP span originally crossed a branch of Rocky Fork Creek. (GPS: N40 10.62 W82 18.36)

Licking County, Ohio   NSPCB 35-45-05

LICKING COUNTY, GIRL SCOUT CAMP OR MERCER OR SHOULTS COVERED BRIDGE (35-45-05). One of two bridges in Licking County with the name of Mercer, this bridge was constructed in 1879 for less than $5 per linear foot. Rebuilt in 2005, the 68-foot bridge spans Wakatomika Creek, which means "laughing waters." (GPS: N40 14.02 W82 15.00)

LICKING COUNTY, GREGGS MILL OR HANDEL COVERED BRIDGE (35-45-06). Nestled in the hills and surrounded by a split-rail fence, this bridge displays the rural charm it did when built in 1881. The 124-foot span is one of five covered bridges that once crossed Wakatomika Creek. A concrete floor and center pier were added later. Gregg's burr mill stood nearby. The span was rebuilt in 1993. (GPS: N40 13.30 W82 14.30)

LICKING COUNTY, MERCER/THURMWOOD COVERED BRIDGE (35-45-07). Once called Johnny Little Covered Bridge in error, it was built in 1875 over Wakatomika Creek by Simon Shrake. It was located at the site of a water-powered sawmill. The arches were removed and the bridge was reinforced with steel in 1963. It succumbed to arson in 1985.

Licking County, McLain or Lobdell Park Covered Bridge (35-45-17). The McLain Bridge, built in 1871, fared better than others, perhaps because a poem was posted on an old sign: "All things save this / have changed within our day, / Beside this quiet road / nestled in these joyous hills, / You point your modest structure / toward the sky, / Unsought and all unthanked / you give us still, / Some fragrance of your peace / as we go by." Bridge lore attributes the poem to builder Frank Phillips, who fashioned the 47-foot, MKP bridge across Lobdell Creek. In the 1940s, siding was removed to make repairs but never replaced. The bridge was abandoned until 1977, when it was moved to Fireman's Park in Alexandria and then renovated. (GPS: N40 05.16 W82 36.51)

LOGAN COUNTY, McCOLLY ROAD COVERED BRIDGE (35-46-01). The 125-foot span was built over the Great Miami River in 1876 by the Anderson Green Company of Sidney, Ohio. The Howe truss cost $13.25 per linear foot to construct. The floor once had to be repaired because someone held a wiener roast on the bridge. It was reinforced with steel in 1958 and then rebuilt in 2000. (GPS: N40 24.07 W83 55.45)

LOGAN COUNTY, BICKHAM OR MIAMI VALLEY PIKE COVERED BRIDGE (35-46-03). Built in 1877 by the South Bridge Company of Toledo, the 94-foot bridge spans the south fork of the Great Miami River on a road leading to O'Connor Landing at the east side of Indian Lake near Russells Point. Indian Lake was formed by a retaining wall on the north edge of Route 33. (GPS: N40 28.46 W83 50.42)

MIAMI COUNTY, ELDEAN ROAD OR ALLEN'S MILL COVERED BRIDGE (35-55-01). James and William Hamilton built this bridge in 1860 for $4,044. White pine lumber was shipped from Michigan for the construction. The two-span, 225-foot structure is the second-longest covered bridge in Ohio and spans the Miami River north of Troy. It was repaired in 1922 and 1936 and completely restored in 2005. (GPS: N40 04.675 W84 12.990)

Old Broad Ford   Miami County, Ohio   35-55-03

MIAMI COUNTY, OLD BROAD FORD COVERED BRIDGE (35-55-03). Built over the Great Miami River near Troy, Ohio, in 1853, major renovations were made in 1869 when arches were added. It is thought that the bridge washed away in the 1913 flood. There were once 102 covered bridges in Miami County.

Calais   Monroe County, Ohio   35-56-01   67-94

MONROE COUNTY, CALIS COVERED BRIDGE (35-56-01). This desolate little bridge stood in the rugged landscape of Monroe County. The area is known as the Switzerland of Ohio because of its rocky landscape. The Calis Bridge in Seneca Township has been gone since 1954.

MONROE COUNTY, SWAZY COVERED BRIDGE (35-56-07). Missing siding bares the truss design of this bridge. Built about 1856 over Clearfork Creek, the 39-foot span was removed in 1964. Monroe County was named for James Monroe, the fifth president of the United States.

MONROE COUNTY, SYCAMORE VALLEY BRIDGE (35-56-11). Also spanning Clear Fork Creek, this 80-foot, MKP bridge was removed in 1968.

MONROE COUNTY, FORAKER TIMBER COVERED BRIDGE (35-56-14). The hill country of this part of the state can be seen behind the bridge. Built across the Little Muskingum River in 1886, the 92-foot, MKP span was repaired by the Works Progress Administration (WPA) in the 1930s and reinforced with steel beams. It was rebuilt in 2005. (GPS: N39 39.33 W81 07.26)

Monroe County, Knowlton or Long or Old Camp Covered Bridge (35-56-18).
Peace and quiet at its best depicts this 192-foot, three-span bridge over the Little Muskingum
River. Built in 1887, it sits high on cut-stone abutments. It is one of two remaining bridges in
the county. (GPS: N39 36.06 W81 09.43)

Okey Ruble   Monroe County, Ohio   35-56-21

Monroe County, Okey Ruble Covered Bridge (35-56-21). Two stark views show the
abandoned 25-foot, single king post bridge over North Fork in Seneca Township. Like many
of the 31 covered bridges once in the county, this one did not survive.

MONTGOMERY COUNTY, GERMANTOWN BRIDGE (35-57-01). Constructed in 1865, this unusual bridge with an inverted bowstring suspension (like Jon Bright No. 2) was always open-sided. The 100-foot span over Little Twin Creek was built by Dayton bridge designer David Morrison. It collapsed twice because of collisions with a threshing machine and an automobile, in 1911 and 1981 respectively. Each time the community rallied to rebuild it. (GPS: N39 37.58 W84 21.90)

Wagoner Ford   Montgomery County, Ohio   35-57-44   67-96

MONTGOMERY COUNTY, WAGGONER FORD COVERED BRIDGE (35-57-44). Built in 1870, this was 1 of 15 covered bridges that once spanned the Great Miami River. An advertisement for paint can be seen above the entrance. Advertising posters were once plastered on covered bridges like today's graffiti. This span was washed away in the 1913 flood.

78

MORGAN COUNTY, PORTER COVERED BRIDGE (35-58-02). Built in 1873, this 65-foot bridge crossed a branch of Meigs Creek near Bristol, Ohio, where it stood until 1977. There were once 58 covered bridges in Morgan County. Strip mining destroyed many bridges; others were submerged in the creation of new dams.

Fairgrounds   Morgan County, Ohio   35-58-32

MORGAN COUNTY, ROSSEAU OR FAIRGROUNDS COVERED BRIDGE (35-58-32). This 58-foot, MKP bridge originally spanned Wolf Creek. In 1953, it was one of the first bridges in Ohio to be preserved by moving from its original location, in this case to the Morgan County Fairgrounds in McConnelsville. The interior of this single-span structure has park benches for the relaxation of fairgoers. (GPS: N39 38.36 W81 50.36)

MORGAN COUNTY, ISLAND RUN (HELMICK MILL) COVERED BRIDGE (35-58-35). This lovely bridge is featured in the author's introduction. Built over the rocky crags of Island Run in 1867, this 74-foot, single MKP span crosses a deep rock-strewn gorge near Eagleport. A natural falls below the bridge makes it one of the most picturesque bridges in Ohio and the perfect spot for a summer picnic. Samuel Price built the bridge for $872. In 2008, it was beautifully restored and an arch added for support. Miriam Wood of the OHBA describes it as a "model preservation project." According to Morgan County engineer Stevan Hook, the cost to renovate the bridge was $407,000. Located in a hollow, this area is much as it was a century ago. The roads leading to the bridge are dirt and gravel-covered. (GPS: N39 43.186 W81 56.534)

Coopermill Road   Muskingum County, Ohio   35-60-07

MUSKINGUM COUNTY, ANDREWS COVERED BRIDGE (35-60-07). Built over Thompson Run in 1892, it was bypassed by a new bridge on CR 71 in 1969. The 60-foot, MKP span was then used as a storage shed. At one time, the county had the third-highest number (167) of covered bridges in Ohio, but only 1 remains.

MUSKINGUM COUNTY, PLEASANT VALLEY COVERED BRIDGE (35-60-30). This unusual bridge had two distinctive spans, a 90-foot QP and a 150-foot Smith truss, resulting in an uneven roofline. The shorter QP span was part of the original bridge. In 1875, the longer Smith span replaced a portion of the QP. Destroyed by a flood in 1959, it was the last covered bridge over the Licking River.

Muskingum County, Johnson Mill (Salt Creek) Covered Bridge (35-60-31). Built in 1876, the 87-foot span is the only remaining Warren truss construction in Ohio. It was built at Johnson's Mill by Thomas Fisher for $8 per linear foot. In 1960, the bridge and two-thirds of an acre were sold for $300 to what is now the Ohio Historic Bridge Association. It was renovated in 1998. (GPS: N39 59.95 W81 50.41)

Muskingum County, Old Y Bridge (35-60-40). Five bridges have spanned where the Muskingum and Licking Rivers meet in a "Y" shape in Zanesville (only one was covered). The first Y Bridge opened in 1814 and was carried away by a flood within six months; the second bridge was declared unsafe in 1831 after 13 years. A popular joke states that directions were once given to a traveler to "go to the middle and turn left."

MUSKINGUM COUNTY, OLD Y BRIDGE (35-60- 40). The third Y Bridge was built as a covered bridge in 1832 by Catherinus Buckingham. It was Buckingham's first and only bridge. It was double-barreled but had the added feature of a covered walkway. It was privately owned and was maintained as a toll bridge until 1868. The tollbooth was in the middle of the bridge. After the covered bridge closed in 1900, a fourth bridge (uncovered and shown below) was constructed in 1902. That bridge was remodeled after the 1913 flood caused major damage. By 1983, it too was declared unsafe. A new fifth bridge was completed in 1984. *Ripley's Believe it or Not* lists the Y Bridge as "the only bridge in the world which you can cross and still be on the same side of the river."

"Y" BRIDGE, ZANESVILLE, OHIO.

61864

MUSKINGUM COUNTY, THIRD STREET OR LOWER OR SOUTH STREET COVERED BRIDGE (35-60-43). Built in 1845 over the Muskingum River, just below the Y Bridge (Upper Bridge), this replaced an earlier crossing destroyed by arson. Allegedly a disgruntled workman set fire to the first bridge to create work for those who were unemployed. The new bridge was a five-span Buckingham truss that was destroyed by the 1913 flood.

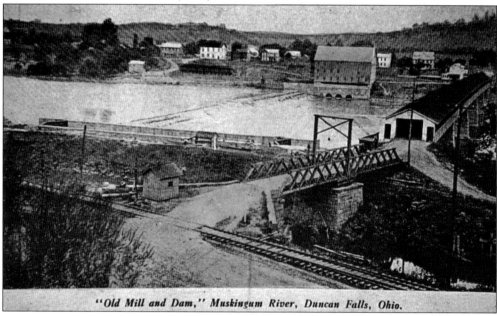

"Old Mill and Dam," Muskingum River, Duncan Falls, Ohio.

MUSKINGUM COUNTY, DUNCAN FALLS COVERED BRIDGE (35-60-47). Featured on the back cover, this 798-foot, Smith truss structure, built in 1864, spanned the Muskingum River at Philo. It was damaged by an ice jam in 1884 and by wind in 1908, only to be swept away in the 1913 flood. The canal lock in the foreground had an iron bridge, which swiveled to allow passage of the boats.

Three

Noble County through Wyandot County

Noble County, Morris or House Covered Bridge (35-61-10). The winter scene is all that remains of the 50-foot, Howe truss span over Beaver Creek. It was near Batesville in the Seneca Lake region and was lost in 1965.

Batesville Noble County, Ohio 35-61-11

NOBLE COUNTY, BATESVILLE COVERED BRIDGE (35-61-11). Noble County once had 112 covered bridges like this one, which was turned out to pasture after years of service. The 48-foot bridge built in 1870 was just south of Batesville and lasted until 1981.

NOBLE COUNTY, CAIN ARCHER COVERED BRIDGE (35-61-29). The 75-foot, MKP bridge was built in 1900 by Beth Rucker, a carpenter from Carlisle. The rustic bridge crossed the east fork of Duck Creek. After 1965 it no longer stood.

NOBLE COUNTY, MANCHESTER COVERED BRIDGE (35-61-33). Standing near an old sycamore tree, this 49-foot, MKP span crosses Olive Green Branch. Built in 1915, it replaced a previous bridge destroyed by the 1913 flood. It was repaired in 1961 and then rebuilt in 2005. (GPS: N39 42.98 W81 37.00)

NOBLE COUNTY, PARRISH COVERED BRIDGE (35-61-34). A refreshing country scene shows the bridge rebuilt in 1914 after the 1913 flood disaster. This 81-foot, MKP span crosses the Sharon Fork of East Olive Creek. It was repaired and painted red in 1964 and rebuilt in 2005. (GPS: N39 42.37 W81 34.96)

NOBLE COUNTY, RICH VALLEY OR FORAKER COVERED BRIDGE (35-61-36 NOW 35-61-104).
Built in 1895, this 65-foot, MKP span also crossed Olive Creek. In 1970, this bridge and the
Park Hill Road Covered Bridge (35-61-40) were torn down and the wood used to build another
44-foot span on the fairgrounds at Caldwell. (GPS: N39 44.53 W81 31.85)

NOBLE COUNTY, DANFORD COVERED BRIDGE (35-61-42). A five-ton weight limit is posted
on this wooden bridge, which is typical of loads old spans can carry. Built in 1875, this 66-foot,
MKP bridge spanned Keith Fork 2.5 miles north of Dungannon. It was removed in the mid-
1990s, because according to the county engineer's office, "It was beyond repair."

NOBLE COUNTY, JOHN STEPHENS COVERED BRIDGE (35-61-65). A farmhouse and barns can be seen near this bridge, which spanned Beaver Creek 2.5 miles southeast of Kennonsburg. It was removed in 1941 when Seneca Lake was created.

NOBLE COUNTY, EAST STREET COVERED BRIDGE (35-61-81). Structures in the town of Belle Valley can be seen behind this bridge, which crossed Wolf Run on Old U.S. 21. A sidewalk for pedestrian safety can be seen to the left of the span.

PERRY COUNTY, PARKS OR SOUTH COVERED BRIDGE (35-64-02). The 58-foot, MKP span crosses a branch of Jonathan Creek in Hopewell Township. William Dean built this bridge in 1883. Between 1874 and 1886, he built 23 Buckingham truss bridges. Dean always built a camber into his bridges, as can be seen in the slight arc in the roofline of this one. (GPS: N39 51.14 W82 16.74)

PERRY COUNTY, HOPEWELL CHURCH COVERED BRIDGE (35-64-03). Crossing Painter's Creek is this trim 55-foot, MKP bridge built in 1874 by Hiram Dennison for $4.85 per linear foot. The Hopewell Church, first organized in 1812, can be seen in the background. (GPS: N39 51.82 W82 16.97)

PERRY COUNTY, CHALFANT COVERED BRIDGE (35-64-04). This six-panel, 66-foot, MKP bridge spanned Painter's Run on State Route 204 in 1878. The above postcard marked the bridge as abandoned; the one below shows it in further decline. It stood until the winter of 1978. Perry County once had 85 covered bridges, which were excellent examples of the MKP construction; 5 remain. Perry County was named for Commodore Oliver Perry, hero of Lake Erie. The county once produced more coal than any other county in Ohio.

Chalfant   Perry County, Ohio   35-64-04

PERRY COUNTY, JACK'S HOLLOW OR KENT'S RUN COVERED BRIDGE (35-64-05). Built in 1879 by William Dean, the 60-foot, MKP bridge suffered fire damage caused by vandals in 1989. It was closed for repairs and then reopened. It is one of four such structures in Perry County that are painted red with white portals. (GPS: N39 54.41 W82 10.09)

PERRY COUNTY, BOWMAN MILL OR REDINGTON COVERED BRIDGE (35-64-06). The 82-foot, MKP bridge was built over Rush Creek in 1859 by Gottlieb Bunzz of Hocking County. In 1987, it was moved to the county fairgrounds. (GPS: N39 43.25 W82 13.47)

PICKAWAY COUNTY, ASHVILLE COVERED BRIDGE (35-65-01). This was the last covered bridge in Pickaway County. The 200-foot span, built across Walnut Creek in 1871, stood for nearly a century before it was removed in 1962.

Circleville Aqueduct   Pickaway County, Ohio   35-65-07

PICKAWAY COUNTY, CIRCLEVILLE AQUEDUCT COVERED BRIDGE (35-65-07). The aqueduct was nothing more than a covered wooden trough filled with water that allowed the canal to cross the river. Cargo boats and passenger packets floated along in the dim water tunnel of the aqueduct, which stood high above the river. In winter, the water in the aqueduct iced over and was used for skating. Built in 1838, the aqueduct was destroyed by fire in 1915.

PIKE COUNTY, BARGER FARM COVERED BRIDGE (35-66-02). This privately owned bridge spanning the Ohio and Erie Canal was likely built in 1832. A trapdoor in the floor of the bridge served as a convenience for farmers to unload grains directly into canal boats under the bridge. It was not maintained and collapsed into the canal bed in 1972.

PREBLE COUNTY, STATE LINE COVERED BRIDGE (35-68-02 OR 14-81-06). Built in 1893, the 111-foot bridge straddled Four Mile Creek in College Corner. One half was in Ohio, while the other half was in Indiana. According to Robert Reed in *Indiana's Covered Bridges,* it was a half-bridge in Indiana since "its upkeep is shared by Preble County, Ohio." A 1937 report lists Ohio covered bridges as 609 ½. It was replaced in 1961.

PREBLE COUNTY, HARSHMAN COVERED BRIDGE (35-68-03). The 104-foot Childs truss was built in 1894 by Everett Sherman, who came to Preble County after the severe storms of 1886 destroyed many bridges. Sherman built 15 bridges during a 10-year period. His contracts always stipulated one-third payment the day of the contract, one-third payment when half-completed, and the balance paid when completed and approved by the county commissioners. (GPS: N39 41.99 W84 46.16)

PREBLE COUNTY, DIXON'S BRANCH COVERED BRIDGE (35-68-04). Built by Everett Sherman in 1887, the 50-foot Childs truss spanned Dixon Branch. Several Childs truss bridges like this one are still standing. It was named for Eli Dixon, the first settler in the area. He moved from Georgia in 1804, the year after Ohio gained statehood. In 1964, the bridge was moved to Civitan Park in Lewisburg. (GPS: N39 50.70 W84 32.13)

Roberts   Preble County, Ohio   35-68-05

PREBLE COUNTY, ROBERT'S COVERED BRIDGE (35-68-05). Advertising posters were plastered on the old view of the bridge. Built in 1829, this is Ohio's oldest covered bridge and the only double-barreled one. Preble County once had five double-lane bridges. The 79-foot, Burr arch span crossing Seven Mile Creek is built of native oak and poplar. The builders were Orlistus Roberts and his 17-year-old apprentice, James L. Campbell. When Roberts died before its completion, Campbell finished the bridge and later married Mrs. Roberts. In 1986, arsonists attempted to burn the bridge, destroying the roof and siding and scorching the trusses. County engineers ultimately restored the bridge in a four-year-long project and moved it to Eaton in 1990. According to county engineer Steve Simmons, covered bridges now have rapid heat rise detectors to thwart arsonists. (GPS: N39 44.37 W84 38.30)

PREBLE COUNTY, BRUBAKER COVERED BRIDGE (35-68-06). The one-lane, 85-foot bridge has carried Aukerman Creek Road over Sam's Run since 1887. The Childs truss span is one of the remaining so-called "S bridges" in Ohio. Since there is an S-curve on either end of the bridge, making it difficult to see oncoming traffic, the sides were left open. (GPS: N39 39.10 W84 32.63)

Winchester   Preble County, Ohio   35-68-07

PREBLE COUNTY, WINCHESTER COVERED BRIDGE (35-68-07). This was the third covered bridge that stood at the same site over Twin Creek on the Lanier and Gratis township line. Built in 1888, it was removed in 1947.

PREBLE COUNTY, LYCURGIS BEAM COVERED BRIDGE (35-68-09). The 85-foot, Childs truss structure, built in 1887, spanned Elkhorn Creek. It was destroyed by arson in 1976. Only 16 bridges were constructed with the Childs truss design—15 were in Preble County and the 16th was constructed by Everett Sherman earlier in Delaware County.

PREBLE COUNTY, TYLER OR SLOANE COVERED BRIDGE (35-68-10). Built over Banta's Fork in 1891, the 118-foot, Childs truss span was removed in 1958 to a private farm, where it was used as a storage shed until the 1980s. Some covered bridges carried a sign that read, "Do Not Drive or Ride Faster than a Walk. $10 fine."

PREBLE COUNTY, CHRISTMAN COVERED BRIDGE (35–68–12). Visions of the holidays are evoked in this snow-covered setting. Built in 1895, this was the next-to-last bridge constructed by Everett Sherman. Spanning Seven Mile creek, the 92-foot bridge was a Childs truss design. The timber dealer's name, Cobbs and Mitchell of Cadillac, Michigan, is still stenciled on interior beams. It was rebuilt in 2008. (GPS: N39 46.22 W84 39.31)

PREBLE COUNTY, GEETING COVERED BRIDGE (35–68–13). Covered bridges were sometimes known as "kissing bridges" because they were places where lovers could meet away from prying eyes. This 100-foot span was built in 1894 over Price Creek near the Old National Road. It is a Childs truss design. (GPS: N39 50.620 W84 35.828)

PREBLE COUNTY, WARNKE COVERED BRIDGE (35-68-14). At 52 feet, this was Everett Sherman's shortest and last Childs truss bridge. Built in 1895, it crosses Swamp Creek. Preble County originally had 50 covered bridges; 7 remain. (GPS: N39 52.43 W84 30.89)

Duffield   Preble County, Ohio   35-68-17

PREBLE COUNTY, DUFFIELD COVERED BRIDGE (35-68-17). This bridge was rebuilt as a 200-foot, two-span bridge by Everett Sherman in 1890. Its predecessor was wrecked by a flood that washed a new channel for Seven Mile Creek. It suffered the same fate in 1933.

PREBLE COUNTY, STOTLER MILL COVERED BRIDGE (35-68-19). The above postcard shows Stotler Mill and Bridge in a painting from the inside of a wooden bowl, which was crafted by a self-taught artist. The two people in the foreground represent the artist's parents. The view below is from April 1910, when a Dayton and Western streetcar left the tracks beside the bridge and plunged into Twin Creek at the eastern edge of West Alexandria. The bridge was a double-barreled Howe truss with huge arches. Built in 1855, it replaced another covered bridge at the same site, which was destroyed when an adjacent mill burned. This bridge was replaced in 1925.

Stotler Mill   Preble County, Ohio   35-68-19

RICHLAND COUNTY, ROME COVERED BRIDGE (35-70-01). This was the county's last covered bridge. It was a 105-foot, Smith truss span built over Black Fork Creek in 1874. The Smith Bridge Company constructed it out of Michigan pine to replace an earlier bridge built in 1857. Rome Bridge was destroyed by arson in 1971. Johnny Appleseed was a frequent visitor to the Richland County area.

ROSS COUNTY, OLD SHOTTS COVERED BRIDGE (35-71-01). David Shotts, a Ross County commissioner, spearheaded a movement to build this bridge in 1870 over Paint Creek. The 278-foot, two-span, Long truss crossing was built by John Gregg and replaced in 1960. The new steel structure is anchored on the ancient piers of the old landmark.

Ross County, Buckskin Covered Bridge (35-71-02). Erected over Buckskin Creek in 1873, the 99-foot, Howe truss span is typical of Ohio covered bridges. Rebuilt in 2006, it is Ross County's only remaining covered bridge of the 92 once constructed there. (GPS: N39 20.04 W83 18.85)

Chillicothe   Ross County, Ohio   35-71-06

Ross County, Bridge Street Covered Bridge (35-71-06). Built at Chillicothe in 1817, this is Ohio's first covered bridge of record. Eli Fox (millwright and shipbuilder) replicated a Theodore Burr bridge constructed earlier in New Jersey. This bridge carried the double roadway over the Scioto River in two 150-foot spans. A third span was added in 1844, creating an uneven roofline. The unusual old bridge was removed by burning in 1886.

Bainbridge   Ross County, Ohio   35-71-07

ROSS COUNTY, SEYMOUR COVERED BRIDGE (35-71-07). The bridge was designed by Lewis Wernwag and built by John Slee in 1840 for the Chillicothe and Milford Turnpike Company. Wernwag's bridge was a two-lane single span. Wernwag used his own patented design for the arched wooden truss. The bridge was located near Bainbridge and crossed Paint Creek. It was removed in 1933 because of abutment failure.

Frankfort Ross County, Ohio 35-71-14

ROSS COUNTY, FRANKFORT COVERED BRIDGE (35-71-14). The bridge was built in 1869 over the north fork of Paint Creek south of Frankfort, where it stood until 1915.

SANDUSKY COUNTY, MULL COVERED BRIDGE (35-72-01). This bridge crosses the east branch of Wolf Creek. Built in 1851, it was originally a single-span named for Amos Mull, who lived nearby. The 100-foot bridge was later expanded into two spans although there is no record of when the concrete pier was added. Bypassed in 1962, the Town lattice construction was renovated in 1990. (GPS: N41 15.65 W83 11.07)

SANDUSKY COUNTY, FREMONT COVERED BRIDGE (35-72-03). Cyrus Williams built this bridge over the Sandusky River in 1841–1842. The wood for the bridge came from a trestle of the Ohio Company in Fremont. The message on the back of the 1912 postcard reads, "Am having a good time from Fremont." Only seven covered bridges were built in the county, but a railroad bridge over the Sandusky River was Ohio's longest timber truss at 1,088 feet.

SCIOTO COUNTY, OTWAY OR BRUSH CREEK COVERED BRIDGE (35-73-15). Of the 84 bridges that were built here, only this one survives. The Smith Bridge Company built the 127-foot span across Brush Creek in 1874. Arches and tension rods were added in 1896. Steel trusses at the end of the bridge replaced the original Smith truss. The bridge was bypassed in 1963. (GPS: N38 51.79 W83 11.40)

SHELBY COUNTY, LOCKINGTON COVERED BRIDGE (35-75-01). Built in 1851, this 183-foot, Long truss bridge crossed the Great Miami River. In the late 1890s, a flood cut a new channel, creating an island around an abutment that required steel pony trusses to be added. In 1963, an ice jam endangering the bridge was blasted away. The last covered bridge in the county succumbed to arson in 1989.

Lorami   Shelby County   35-75-02

SHELBY COUNTY, DAWSON COVERED BRIDGE (35-75-02). This grainy photograph was shot in 1925 of the bridge that spanned Loramie Creek between the towns of Houston and Dawson. Advertising posters are peeling off the portals. The bridge was torn down in 1939 as part of a WPA project.

SUMMIT COUNTY, EVERETT ROAD COVERED BRIDGE (35-77-01). The only remaining bridge in Summit County was built over Furnace Run in 1870. The Smith construction is 100 feet long. In 1975, flooding caused one abutment of the bridge to collapse. The timbers were pulled from the creek, marked, and stored for rebuilding. In 1986, the National Park Service reconstructed the bridge with mostly new timbers. (GPS: N41 12.24 W81 35.00)

SUMMIT COUNTY, BOZTZUM COVERED BRIDGE (35-77-05). This bucolic view of the bridge depicts children with a farm animal standing between them. It spanned the Cuyahoga River on Bath Road near Riverview. Summit County recorded only 18 covered bridges.

OLD BOTZUM — COVERED BRIDGE
STOOD ON BATH ROAD NEAR RIVERVIEW

TRUMBALL COUNTY, NEWTON FALLS COVERED BRIDGE (35-78-01). The only remaining covered bridge in Trumball County was built in 1831 to cross the East Branch of the Mahoning River. It is the second-oldest covered bridge in Ohio. The Town truss construction spans 117 feet. It is Ohio's only historical covered bridge with a sidewalk, which was constructed in 1921 so schoolchildren could cross safely. (GPS: N41 11.29 W80 58.26)

TRUMBALL COUNTY, BRACEVILLE OR DIEHL COVERED BRIDGE (35-78-02). Located just west of Warren, this bridge also spanned the Mahoning River. In 1878, a contract was agreed upon for a "new bridge at Mrs. Diehl's." Robert Stewart built the fully covered bridge for $12 per linear foot. The Howe truss bridge was destroyed by a fire of undetermined origin in 1959.

TRUMBALL COUNTY, WEST COVERED BRIDGE AT NEWTON FALLS (35-78-03). Built in 1856 over the west branch of the Mahoning River, it replaced an earlier span built in 1832. It was a two-lane, open-sided bridge with a roofed sidewalk on both sides. Advertising posters can be seen on the portals. The Historic American Building Survey made detailed drawings of the span in the 1930s. It was replaced in 1943.

Braceville   Trumbull County, Ohio   35-78-02R

Newton Falls,   Trumbull County, Ohio

UNION COUNTY, POTTERSBURG OR UPPER DARBY COVERED BRIDGE (35-80-01). The 94-foot span (1868) is one of four surviving covered bridges constructed by Russell L. Partridge, the county's premier bridge builder. Partridge constructed over 33 wooden bridges in his home county. It was moved 3,000 feet south of its original location in 2006. A new covered bridge was built in its place. (GPS: N40 14.47 W81 31.77)

UNION COUNTY, SPAIN CREEK COVERED BRIDGE (35-80-02). This charming little bridge was built over Spain Creek around 1870. The Partridge truss is 64 feet long. It was rehabilitated in 1988–1989. County engineers constructed two new covered bridges in 2006. (GPS: N40 14.12 W83 31.52)

UNION COUNTY, WINGET ROAD OR TREACLE CREEK OR CULBERTSON COVERED BRIDGE (35-80-03). Built in 1868, the 94-foot Partridge span now crosses Treacle Creek, where it was moved from an unknown prior location. The patented Partridge truss features braces and counter braces resting against a bifurcated metal or wooden shoe. (GPS: N40 08.30 W83 27.13)

UNION COUNTY, AXE HANDLE ROAD OR BIGELOW OR LITTLE DARBY BRIDGE (35-80-04). This single-span covered crossing was built in 1873 by Russell L. Partridge. The 102-foot bridge crosses Little Darby Creek. In the 1930s, roofed windows were cut into the sides to improve safety and visibility. (GPS: N40 06.97 W83 25.50)

UNION COUNTY, LONDON ROAD OR REED BRIDGE (35-80-05). Built around 1870, this 155-foot, Partridge truss bridge spanned Big Darby Creek. It was said to be one of the best-preserved and most picturesque covered bridges. However, as researchers stepped away after examining the bridge in August 1993, to their dismay it suddenly collapsed into the creek. Fortunately no one was injured in the mishap.

VINTON COUNTY, MOUNT OLIVE OR GRAND STAFF COVERED BRIDGE (35-82-04). George Washington Pilcher built this (QP) truss design in 1875. Pilcher, also a stonemason, built six of the QP bridges in Vinton County. Ohio has few bridges of the QP design. This shady scene shows the 48-foot span over Middle Branch of Salt Creek. (GPS: N39 17.177 W82 35.320)

VINTON COUNTY, BAY OR TINKER COVERED BRIDGE (35-82-05). Constructed in 1876 by Graves and Scott Builders, the 63-foot, double MKP truss bridge once crossed Little Raccoon Creek north of Hamden. The cost to build it new was $9.50 per linear foot. In 1966, it was moved for $2,000 to the fairgrounds, where it now spans a small pond. (GPS: N39 16.19 W82 28.47)

VINTON COUNTY, GEER'S MILL OR HUMPBACK OR PONN'S COVERED BRIDGE (35-82-06). The unusual 165-foot, three-span, MKP bridge with an arch was built in 1874, replacing a previous bridge over Raccoon Creek. Martin McGrath and Lyman Wells were hired as contractors for $1,898. The arching of this structure makes it unique. It has a camber of 19 inches in both the top and bottom chords. (GPS: N39 02.89 W82 22.59)

Arbaugh   Vinton County, Ohio   35-82-07

VINTON COUNTY, EAKIN MILL OR ARBAUGH COVERED BRIDGE (35-82-07). This bridge, similar to Humpback Bridge, was built in 1870 a few miles upstream on Raccoon Creek. It was also known as Geer's Mill Bridge because it was near the mill of Henry Geer, brother of Jacob Geer for whom the other humpback bridge was named. The road to the 111-foot, double MKP truss crossing is closed. (GPS: N39 10.29 W82 20.20)

VINTON COUNTY, COX COVERED BRIDGE (35-82-10). Known as the county's shortest bridge at just 40 feet, it spans Brushy Fork. It was built in 1884 by Diltz and Steel. The QP design differs from the MKP because of a separate horizontal beam (chord) between the two vertical trusses in the center panel. In 1992, it was moved a few feet to a new concrete foundation. (GPS: N39 21.96 W82 27.64)

WARREN COUNTY, SPRINGBORO COVERED BRIDGE (35-83-?). The message on the back of this undated postcard states that it is an "old covered bridge near Springboro." Several bridges spanned Clear Creek near this location. The last one collapsed in the 1930s.

WASHINGTON COUNTY, RANSOM LANE COVERED BRIDGE (35-84-01). Originally this MKP bridge, built in 1894, spanned Aldridge's Run. In 1967, the 44-foot bridge was moved to a park and dry land in Marietta, where it stood until 1974. Washington County is located at the confluence of the Ohio and Muskingum Rivers. Marietta is one of the oldest cities in Ohio, where early settlers replenished supplies before heading further north or west.

WASHINGTON COUNTY, SHINN COVERED BRIDGE (35-84-03). Built in 1886, this bridge is one of the few remaining examples of the Burr king post arch. Theodore Burr patented his idea in 1804. The 98-foot span was built over the West Branch of Wolf Creek because of the near drowning of a child of the Charles Shinn family. Charles Shinn assisted in the construction of the bridge. (GPS: N39 27.77 W81 45.67)

WASHINGTON COUNTY, HENRY COVERED BRIDGE (35-84-06). The attractive wooded setting is near the West Branch of the Little Hocking River. This span succeeded a footbridge, from which a child drowned on her way to school. Built by E. B. Henderson in 1894, the 45-foot, MKP span is constructed of chestnut wood. (GPS: N39 22.99 W81 47.09)

WASHINGTON COUNTY, ROOT COVERED BRIDGE (35-84-08). This 1878 charmer is a reminder of bygone days. The 65-foot span crosses the south branch of the Little Hocking River. This bridge uses the Long truss system patented by Col. Stephen Long. The majority of the Long truss designs were built in southern Ohio, most likely because Long had an agent named Stephen Daniels, who served as a contractor. (GPS: N39 20.56 W81 45.24)

WASHINGTON COUNTY, WILLIAMS OR MARTIN COVERED BRIDGE (35-84-09). Built around 1880, this 69-foot, MKP bridge spanned the west branch of the Little Hocking River. A flood washed it away in 1963, and it was replaced by a steel structure.

WASHINGTON COUNTY, HARRA COVERED BRIDGE (35-84-11). This 95-foot, Long truss bridge was constructed in 1878 over the south branch of Wolf Creek. It was erected by Rolla Merydith, a Washington County builder. Many of his bridges used yellow poplar, which was about 50¢ more per linear foot to build than oak. Merydith earned between $6.50 and $7.17 per linear foot to build the bridge. (GPS: N39 29.23 W81 38.90)

WASHINGTON COUNTY, BELL COVERED BRIDGE (35-84-12). In 1888, E. B. Henderson also built this 59-foot bridge of MKP design to span the southwest fork of Wolf Creek. (GPS: N39 25.85 W81 40.58)

WASHINGTON COUNTY, MILL BRANCH COVERED BRIDGE (35-84-17). Located just north of Belpre, the single-span, 65-foot, MKP bridge crossed the Little Hocking River. In 1980, it was moved to the Barlow fairgrounds. (GPS: N39 23.96 W81 40.05)

WASHINGTON COUNTY, HILDRETH OR HILLS COVERED BRIDGE (35-84-24). This lovely 122-foot crossing spans the Little Muskingum River near Marietta. It cost $13 per linear foot to build in 1878. Named for its designer William Howe, the Howe truss system used iron rods for the tension members in place of the wooden truss verticals that had been used by the Long truss system. (GPS: N39 25.64 W81 21.67)

WASHINGTON COUNTY, COW RUN COVERED BRIDGE (35-84-25). This bridge also crossed the Little Muskingum River where it was joined by Cow's Run north of Marietta. Built in 1872, the single span was 150 feet long and constructed of the Long truss design, which used wood for the verticals. Col. Steven Long sued William Howe for patent infringement but lost. The bridge was removed in late 1967.

WASHINGTON COUNTY, HUNE COVERED BRIDGE (35-84-27). This timber crossing was built in 1879 by Rolla Merydith. The 128-foot, Howe Truss crossing was named for the Hune family, who settled along the Little Muskingum River. The stone for the abutments was quarried and the yellow poplar hewn from the Hune farm. Merydith boarded with the Hune family while building the span. It was renovated in 1998. (GPS: N39 30.63 W81 15.02)

WASHINGTON COUNTY, RINARD COVERED BRIDGE (35-84-28). The Smith Bridge Company built this 130-foot span in 1876 just upstream from the Hune Bridge. It replaced a previous bridge (1870) that had washed away in a flood. In 2004, the new span was also destroyed in the aftermath of flooding caused by Hurricane Ivan. The bridge was rebuilt in 2006. (GPS: N39 32.21 W81 13.35)

Michaels   Wyandot County, Ohio   35-88-02   67-91

WYANDOT COUNTY, MICHAELS OR BRODMAN COVERED BRIDGE (35-88-02). Built in the 1850s, this bridge crossed Tymochtee Creek in Salem Township; it stood until 1946. Wyandot County once had 21 covered bridges, but only 2 are still standing.

121

Parker Covered Bridge, 5½ Miles N. E., Upper Sandusky, Ohio—Built 1873

WYANDOT COUNTY, PARKER COVERED BRIDGE (35-88-03). The single-span, 172-foot, Howe truss bridge was built in 1873 to cross the Sandusky River. It was built by J. C. Davis of Marion, Ohio. Vandals set fire to the bridge in 1991, causing the south end to fall into the river. It was rebuilt in 1992. (GPS: N40 54.18 W83 14.69)

WYANDOT COUNTY, SWARTZ COVERED BRIDGE (35-88-05). Crossing the Sandusky River, this fine Howe truss design was built in 1878. The 96-foot span was rebuilt in 1994. (GPS: N40 46.24 W83 10.15)

Four

COVERED BRIDGE
FESTIVALS

ASHTABULA COUNTY COVERED BRIDGE FESTIVAL. This festival is held the second full weekend of October at the Ashtabula Fairgrounds in Jefferson, Ohio. The festival provides a covered bridge driving tour map of 17 covered bridges (12 historical and 5 new). The tour is divided into two parts, each covering a little over 65 miles; guided tours are available. The festival offers activities for children, official souvenirs, crafts, entertainment, historical vehicles, contests, parades, and food.

ASHTABULA COUNTY, SMOLEN–GULF COVERED BRIDGE (35-04-64). It is the most impressive of the Ashtabula tour. The new bridge was dedicated in 2008 and is the longest covered bridge in the United States at 613 feet in length. During the festival activities are held at each location.

ASHTABULA COUNTY, NETCHER ROAD COVERED BRIDGE (35-04-63). This new bridge was built in 1998. It is an inverted Haupt bridge with arches. It is painted bright red and is more decorative than some of the historical bridges.

UNION COUNTY COVERED BRIDGE FESTIVAL. This festival is held the second weekend in September. Two-hour covered bridge bus tours stop by four historical bridges, two new bridges, and one historical steel truss bridge. Participants may also follow their own tour with a map that takes them on a 36-mile journey. Those with GPS navigational systems will find eight geocaching point stashes for a treasure hunt along the tour route (available only during the festival). Some of the following activities take place in Marysville, Milford Center, Plain City, Unionville Center, and North Lewisburg: presentations about the bridges; a festival fair with crafts, antiques, and food; entertainment; childrens' activities; a five-kilometer run/walk; souvenir sales; demonstrations; a Civil War encampment; and a car rally.

UNION COUNTY, NEW UPPER DARBY, OR POTTERSBURG NO. 2 COVERED BRIDGE (35-80-61). The new bridge was built of the Pratt truss design in 2006. This span sits on the site of the old Pottersburg Bridge, which was moved just 3,000 feet south of this location. It crosses Big Darby Creek on North Lewisburg Road. (GPS: N40 14.95 W83 32.01)

UNION COUNTY COVERED, BUCK RUN ROAD COVERED BRIDGE (35-80-62). One of the new bridges built in 2006 over Big Darby, this span features a Pratt truss design. (GPS: 40 12.60 W83 29.32)

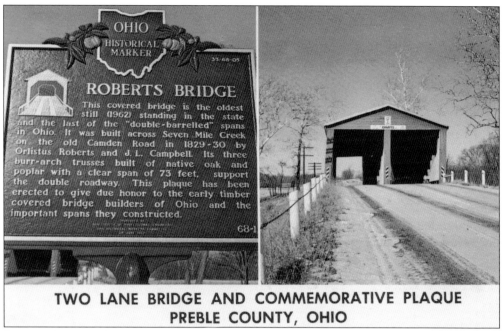

TWO LANE BRIDGE AND COMMEMORATIVE PLAQUE
PREBLE COUNTY, OHIO

PREBLE COUNTY COVERED BRIDGE POKER RUN AND BIKE RIDE. The poker run is held in September and features ale tasting, food and entertainment, and exhibits at the Preble County Historical Society Center in Eaton. The Buckeye Bridge Bike Ride takes place in late June and is a bike ride and five-kilometer run/walk to seven covered bridges.

Y BRIDGE ARTS FESTIVAL, ZANESVILLE, OHIO. The Y Bridge Arts Festival is held the second weekend in August on the historical Y Bridge. Activities include heritage demonstrations, arts and crafts, food, and entertainment.

DISCOVER THOUSANDS OF LOCAL HISTORY BOOKS FEATURING MILLIONS OF VINTAGE IMAGES

Arcadia Publishing, the leading local history publisher in the United States, is committed to making history accessible and meaningful through publishing books that celebrate and preserve the heritage of America's people and places.

Find more books like this at
www.arcadiapublishing.com

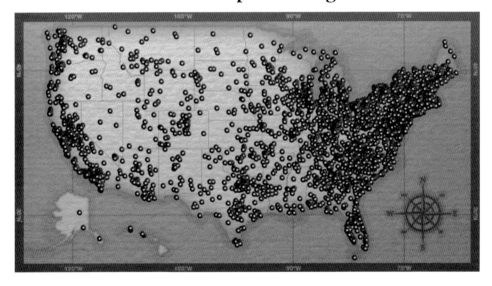

Search for your hometown history, your old stomping grounds, and even your favorite sports team.

MADE IN THE USA